ABSENCES

Poetry

MICHAEL AARON KAMINS

Copyright © 2014 Michael Aaron Kamins
All rights reserved.

ISBN: 1497523036
ISBN 13: 9781497523036

ACKNOWLEDGEMENTS

Special thanks are due to the following individuals for reading various drafts of the manuscript and assisting in the book's final design: John David Ebert, Terri James, Chris Boyd, Abigail Rose Marsicano, and Jacques de Beaufort

CONTENTS

Structures
I. Lines   1
II. Globes   17
III. Codes   33

Annex   51

Afterword by John David Ebert   53

LINES

ABSENCES

SOLELY lines & beyond that nothings. take this string unstrung. link-in this line webbed absence to absence. come thru this fiber-optic dermis. measure. fly lines bio luminously dipped deep into abyss disappearance. or rather sift thru & after. go telepresence gone beaming dreamspeed on this or that other line. nightline. turning starword or otherward this palmtime deathline. lastly solely & of the w/out-ends

SOMEWHERE & after the dividing line of the world's night. this line this a measured quantum between world & abyss. from absence to absence. decided by line upon line. or a flight-line disentangle from this travel surreptitiously the starpaths of the sacred grid

ABSENCES

REWINDLINES. archaic traces. activated time pools. ancient. ever absent present pulses. residues. dregs of desert ebbs. weird wraiths streaming telepathies. beamed sharp from Sirius. desire & absence. rainbowlines thru flashflood. liquefied topologies. all highspeedlines of ever exoduses. unplugged lines of warnings. flash null the signal lines. the inevitable desert mantle mobile. superluminal astral-hooked to portablecity. intertubed thru absences. and rubicund becomings violence on-the-roadlines high. ever-resinous condensing spaces. eventhorizon & astrallines. poliswires. electrified. residues of Egypt. of parallel lines pressed reptileheads. of tentacular city entangling desertminds. absences. and suffocating pools of time. linedeep-in inflatable oasis &-out direct TVline maya to mirages. and-in. deathlines of the crushing EYEmachine. wheels grinding desert bones. into pastes for fixing lines. and blue glues for making time. all today & intertubed thru to

LURID beams. tracings these of traces of the continuity of nothings. holes unplugged. lines these disentangle the measurer from point to null. rings. glow. and scry these pathways on this horizontal tree. so to embrace. island-. by gushing light worlds these tiny open. giant rainbowlights inside

ABSENCES

EARTHLINES radically withdraw enigmas. blackhearts of stars. absences. and evade fingers of buzzing eyes. allspace & times scanning to & fro. w/ lines jutting forth & flickering-out. absence. the irrepressible burble of fade inside-absence-out. and flash lines thru fallen circles of myriad shadow geometries. gone & away worlds gone to absences suck lines into abysses of abyssal sidereal black. lines flirting w/ absence linedeep in deeps of diminishing returns of depth

MICHAEL AARON KAMINS

LIGHTLINES of FRWYs neon being-chains downthru tunneled freetime on highspeedlines trackdown now the beating one-&- zero in the broken heart of being in the Absences. nightlines polarized current dawns pale latelight & gone

ABSENCES

ABSENCES & powerline webs. vestigial echoes of being. mutating lines. in satellite-nets. ancient veinline circulating western swamps. channels of oil w/ timelines to sinkholes. awakening faultlines turnings. vast parking-structures of absent goldmines. w/ tunneled lines to a vanished core. electrified grids. absences. or worldrounding maps suffocating. nows. highspeedlines thru disappearances. plug-ins compressions opened deep gones & out-thru doubly negated nightlines of absence. and vast distance collapsed. w/ lightspeed paradoxes of selfs supersurpassed. and littered in the pasttime of the lightline. enlining ghost HYWYs. bluelines of hypothermia tracing heatwaves of Hollywood. ruptured celestial sidewalks of vestigial stars. or dimming archaic residues constellated by invisible lines. or echoes w/in an echo. of Aether. flattruth of line & disappearance. flatworm spiraling absence. digesting time. w/ lines of night tracing desperate light

MEMORY. mosaics. tendrils. green disappearances. etheric visions. reptilian violence. pale night. black & white. lines. traces of evaporated memories. diaphanous mansions in cesspools of times. lines mutating into multiplicities of animal eyes of blackholes. opened closures of seeings. of evaporations. prismatic splittings. of nows. all streaming lines screaming in hypnoidal black/white opaque nightmares. hyperactive. black. door. white. twisted. lines of powered amethysts their unearthly opacity their lines their memories & abyss w/ supersensible lines of tele-visions. of primordial violence. of obsidian. of night. of spiral-regressed serpentine worldlines timespace enframed the cosmos interwoven of living lines of electrical beings. bright dims of buzzing grids revealings all standings & reserves. sleeplight sculptured nightstoned & from the elsewheres. arks arrive on floodlines in opaque night. gathering memory & absence of goneworlds. arks trailing lines of departure into green disappearances. and new violence. into green disappearances. and new violence

ABSENCES

HORIZONS. gridlines. irreparably televisual. out-here of the desert-scrapped all space & times. trashed blocks of silver. link up & under the gones. thru celebrity ghostshards. so evanescent & longed-for. finally. lines solely & neon. vacancies. amber'd livingdeads. of that achieved there. world. that echo w/out cause. and from an abscess. irredeemably lunar. but here. all tomorrows today. irremediably. remainder. scums. denuded nows. of hyperzeros. lines. whirls. absences of absences. or otherwise lines. swirls. and immense ebbs of sunken time. wormloop'd viral & absent. spiderlines between time & time. and phonelines between absence to absence. and line to lines

VOIDED blackhole-headed inmate sketches lines on desertwall of occult entrance to invisible carnival. surfaces of troubled foam zones hotpink & electriceel. psyberchannel sexline surfing linetrance traced in flight from the gones. synesthesia dispersals. fire pixels. evacuates shiftworlds. of hiflats & absence magnets. incinerating total lines & gone

ABSENCES

LINKED in/out of arcadelines of wish-machine mazes. petition patron djinn playing 24/7 the rolling 4/EX over alltime & earths. flat-pressed thunderous. and flatlined-thru lines lux. and telepresences of the worlds the gones & aways in absentia-lightenings disclosed instantaneously. forgotten

ZEBRALINES. omni mirrored all tomorrows today. zig zagged bioluminescence & static grid shimmerings. snakes & ladders. lines interlaced wheels & spirals. spinning geometric panels zipping psychoid-out-of-telepresence light & headlines. superluminals thru hyperlink-flows absences & times. in the mythic-floodlight recurrings compress series series & of vacancies. parallels encroachings & aways of storms deserts ubiquitous & gnawing at all timelines worldround us. still astral hooked to a broken moon w/lines fried at the tips reach we into the absences all hooked-up & resonating w/ light

ABSENCES

ICEVOIDS. silverlines. timetangled voids. and acidlines. timefree w/out now. trackdown linedeep in deep & out. on the pulse. lines hyperout & off. trackdown now the beating off/on in the electronic heart. in the broken. of AYIN. and out. silverline congested noise. acidtime. whirring hydraulics out of voids. mechanized enlined & time-captured. broken heart of pulselines. triggerfinger deep on the pulse of the wishmachine. gones these gods epiphanic djinn machinenets stars absences & abscessed line twisting downtown hierarchy of blood loa exchanged interminably in icegrid voidtime speedlight eating lines into rings

PHOTOLUMINOUS liquids. air & light. error over linked spiralgrid core vanished under. hot on the pulselines. shot dead gones & dazzle nulls. flattened hierarchies stratify heres. layers cringing biogenous plasmas. postplanet earths rapidly miniaturizing becoming spinning dim antiques in cosmic maws. nothings. gones. lines interstellar break beings in blitzspeed flatlined fast in astral hotels shot-off the old HWY-line backwards to ooze. buzzing constellation fossils. satellized zodiacs webover earths managing all beinglines. in-grid down w/out & in-deep negated & timecringing wasted mutants parse thru electric eelgrids all litup & dialing-out in duress in duress. all lines spacetime things always being always eaten away & into the gones into the gones. parallels. repeats. out

GLOBES

ABSENCES

GLOBES gleaming turn-in Absentia. there severe spheres. dim-up. and puff-in. toward implosion. swaying gleams thru w/ins. globewide this serpentine desert. that cold network of astral spheres. derealings & imploded star aparts englobe & glow. deathglobe & lunar globes. hierarchies of ghosts. in an ecology of globes. gleaming sways. congeal & globe. their ghostorgans. organglobes & ghostlined. multiplying polar zones. night & fire. and absence. of excised bones. take this way's sways & glow opened closing. thru trouble. absence. and empire. out sphere w/out air. bubble w/out water. globes w/out here

GLOBES w/ bones excised. blackhole anatomies. exposed in absentia open. closed. absence of absent orbs. ghost-globes w/ spinning organs. blue glues. of bones ground. globes X-rayed-in. skeletons lightened. boneless globes. X-rayed-out. implode. in betweens. free of ways intestines annexed. in betweens. taxidermist of spheres setting-off dead presences into implosion. diaphanous membranes glowing insides of lightspeed circulatings. imploded flat purely pounded telepathic web-ghosts bone exchanging. disappearance spheres etheric wires. vascular disintegrators. incised egg. exhales vapor blues. translucent spheres. DayGlow veins. omniscient networks circulating oils neons & silver liquid crystal invisible by day/against night. array. and collection. into global skeleton. red X-rayed nothings. absence or abscess. worlds of trashed origami. in arctic void sucked digitalsphere w/ viral lines. overall. hollow. communicating vessels. of astral webs. lightnings vanished globe residues. archaic traces. of ghost immune-systems. sparkle & fadeout. and down. stricken in absentia terrible drastic crawling dead from shells. all

ABSENCES

HOLLYWOODLINES hollow-out enormous gold globes. gleaming. photogenic. mansions of absence homes. malibuglobes globs of time. diaphanous globes w/ phosphorescent bones. organ transplants from globe to globe. cosmetic. spherical. and revolving. palatial chandelier. pale light of disappearances. and dust. valleyglobe of redundancies. of nothings. flightlines from globe to globe. tracked. transposed into fixed zones & winding immobilized. PCH trafficline. globes. timeimploded celluloidglobes. of black&white cinemalines. fading. sunset filmstrip. globes. crystalline & concealing. absences. w/ iconglobes & globeclones. etheric foams shoot. surge. and burn. thru luminous veins of globes. coronary bypass flash of global fadings. and unusual foam globes foaming

IN mercurio. globes erode implode melt & explode into slags blobs & medial blurred chunks & globs. transgenderized in speedlight. mercurius immersed down lava liquefaction. low down so. shot up thru exospheric foam so w/ radioactive glow. Event Horizon quicksilver light-thru electrified aperture. or ruptured spheres sparkles forth spill. captured. standings of metals & aethers. transient iceglobes. bipolar core glitters. nows. unplugged. and in vertigo-dwells. spinning globus glimmers all tomorrows today. on our wall of dialed memorycrystal. forlorn in forget & wasted in lambent pale floodlight clamor. red globe/sapphire sphere. in/out immemorial abgrund black. embattled. ancient sidereal apparatus turned by angels irreparable brokens. fallen moons from glass spheres on which the stars rotate. critically cracked greenhouse case. squall-lined snowglobe ripped from closed hands. violently opened. globes in mercurio. melting slags. absence drags

ABSENCES

GLOBES. dimensions narrowed & defined lunar steeped live in simulation deep. opalescent glowings & gone violent phantasm absent. and null. whorled mysterium disappearances steeped live. narrowings defined golden broken open globes. and gones. deepspace aways & times flit thru-in absentia out of luna sleeplit simulation deeps deep & gone

POLYGLOBES. geocentric ghosts. popshot molecules. flat veins of constellation fossils. negated cosmoses. reversible bubble double-negative being in absentia. drug-globes w/ skullcults & trafficlines. and being metabolized in narcosphere. high. ghostpoliced. and pulverized. in absentia. electrochemical-circles. in fullglobal withdrawal. in metabolites of absence out. rubberdoubles detoxify & ejaculate. in negated unrealglobe. of ghostforms & alienfrosts. in fuckwebs of instantdeath. in afterlifenets of sex/death phantasies. at-homeglobe arcades of prostitution. w/ crippling prosthetics & husks of time. in absentia. of slipping mantles of exposedglobes. in permanent hypothermic catastrophe. frozen bubbles & quasicrystal globes of extraterrestrial origin. in greenlit zones of capsuled lunacy. global profiteers of war. prophets of deep abground. and dealers of absence. in sleeplight. of absentee globelords. proliferating hypodermic deepfreeze. in absentia astralrings & alien deathglobes. allnight intercourse & mourning rigor mortis. accumulating absences. hallucinatory singularities & paucity of forms. in major terrorspheres.

ABSENCES

and minor medial recessed solaces. all
stuck w/pins&needles. of new vicarious
voodoos. in absentia & old cartoons of
being

MICHAEL AARON KAMINS

IN absentia gleam subtle tents wells of shadow i-deep beneath residual rains of zodiacal rings invisible nets imploded globes hellbent held suspended invoids. and out

ABSENCES

CAPSULES of absence. swallow. us. beaming in/out timespiral link. go gone. ghostly thru the absences. rotating reversal of future thru now. image-vaunted for controlled disposal in orbital-space. worlds go. gone out-of-business. globes close down. withdrawn in. lightening capital. absence capsules digestives of globs of time. globes doubly negated shift tableaus lightwired into instances of extinct time. absences. of desert wendigo gone blizzard. of Santa Ana's. sick & lizard. wind whorls absence worlds. globes excised bones in permanences jostle dead neons w/in summer Xmas globular spaceship-lit gones & aways. standstills the global parade at speed of twilight dawns. in reverse permanences. of globes

DEATHGLOBES twilight climes monstrous. gones. in reverse permanences. erosions of time & space imploded. gones. tomorrow today yellowish terrorconditioned spheres. of telekinetic foams. collapsed globes. gelb all & gone. sidereal nightmare panopticon all-time jihad absence & gonesick w/ downtown amarillo fever ghostglobes & broken bubbles. irreparable. and gone. skeletal peoples. and mutant fingers on muted pulses of the ark. out ins resinous everyellow allreversed dawn

ABSENCES

SOLUBLE spheres. vanishings. collapse. open. vast voidlights thundering thru all nowheres in shevirah. incandescent. absent. postsolar superearths. light. drained zodiacs & dangling from our broken dome. darkmouths from of the w/ins of all things eat the reals away. vast voidlights thundering thru the all eaten away & into the gones

MICHAEL AARON KAMINS

GLOBES rupture. north of now & subzero. a vessel gone. bad. of a life. gone. northnow & terror. globe. of brutal security metal. and electrical tentacles. north & absent. terrible desolation in everpresent twilight inside-absence-out

ABSENCES

DESOLATION tourists. postglobe. in the twilight of places the surest ways to the desert of. your life now mortally held. unsheathed & sheathed w/ heavenly lights & speeds of. buzzing bubbles. banished ghosts of. lost globes derealed. raise imaginary doubles. of earths. satellighted. the surest ways afterglobes. of the desert. glows. winding westward shadowtours. of the absences. everpresent in twilight from abscess from absence. astral Ferriswheels skeletal sphere pinball worlds invisible carnival in twilight-place under. vacancy-glitter. missionaries of blackholes. promise the surest. ways to the desert. being yours & life's today electrospherical inward-space weird desolate light & near

GLOBES. turnings. vacancies. aions. gleamings. last wisps evaporating reality. unplugged okeanos. globes degirdled sea dry serpent bones disintegrate last wisps evaporating aions. swaying vacancies today's tomorrows last ghosts gleamings of serpent girdled globes & nowhere here nows nos or globes where earths absorb. in absentia. globes. begone & away i-deep in abyss. and out. everyring shed everything but absently come wilderness back. and nows forlorn in forget & intercordial gnawed to gones into. this late-knowing of discord-ins & out-ons that fastforward implosive-of-all. over. darkened Imagination rest you there. graved & Superstitious Sphaere

CODES

ABSENCES

CODES. gods. absences. betwixt glitters in disappearance matrix of medial blurs. twittering icons flash off on in heimarmene & hover over voidlight. codes. etheric hexagons of flicker-. architecture. of the gones. gods. codes. deep-i in absentia ads. apps. signs. out. twinkling on zapkey scramble codes off. all tomorrows codes today x y zs. in sublime machine modes twisting darkmatter codes inferno inhaler of dreams & stars. outhere perimeter & apex stunned by the codethunder & dismantled. on. whisper a last evaporating word deadstarward. off. despite still bit finger-signaling these glimmering last embers of meaning

QUICKSILVER. codes. technopathic evocations. mercury liquefied. crystalizes. preternatural intelligences. phantasmagoria of plastic forms. glitter & reflect all-tomorrows-today the paradisiacal light-thru our living inferno. into our timespaces. all. and thru the faces myriad. pretend. w/ new magic. codes. passwords to presence living disappearances. codes. to conjure icons from astrallight & dead inferno. codes. for to invoke the codenames of shimmering daemons. codes. to scry the machinery of destiny in silver vision. and to exhume fossilized globes from chasms absences. at finger new codes. for to trigger the world's automatic disappearance

ABSENCES

UP in the air. history decodes. here. the lightening made that lights up the sunken night. flickers. neon. to know. for the down-there the codes the holes in the screen of the dome of the night are constellated into the codes of zodiacal rule. the globe turns into its double its other. inverted. up. no. under. so. this world evaporated by code & synthetic lightbeam. remains an abscess for an eye in the face of being

OFF. on. etheric matrix. of absence. off. codings textual. cool saturn controlcodes. w/touch & beamed texts. beep on buzz. off neural texts. on. off territorialized telepathy. on superluminal sync. and global signal off. saturn codes on. off textual territory of blue hypnoscodes on. telepathic forest of plugged-in textural desertglobes off. on w/ cybernetic saturnmind controlcodes. off collapsing & reverted into saturnine presence on. absence off. on supraphosphenic skeletal territories. of diaphanous skinmaps. off cryptographic absencemaps. on gamma wave encrypted graphs off. on programmed LEDs of being. off w/modes of hallucination on. off absence. neuralblue on. saturnbrain. off w/ touchcodes on. off & textural maps of real absence windows on absences into evaporated houses. off bluecodes of disposed stimuli under. saturnsign & absence raveled on. saturn codes. reign globes. programmed haste into hyperspatial numerals. off. syntactic cortical partitions. of eventfossil on. postsolar phaseshifts. of coolblue codespaces. lunar absent & otherwise off. w/passwords. deathcyphers & agecodes on. sexnumbers & zodiacal

ABSENCES

birth. markings. off. interminable +/- lifedeath sigils on. off & blue superluminal hotlines on. syntaxing saturn. submolecular. endless tape. worm. loops. spun saturn tongue off. terrible prescient spaces. speedprogam on. off absences. obstructions. of midline & lifelight passages on. ectoplasmic hierarchies. of vast etheric nets off. on tentacular calculators. of satellit absence & webs of ghost algebra off. vapor globes. and alembics of saturnbrain. of octopicontrollers on. off submolecular endless tapeloops. unspooled wormcode. of saturn tongue on. bipolar blued tattooed w/ disappearing ink. in aqua permanens. w/suprasensible script. in aqua permanens

MICHAEL AARON KAMINS

GATES of Pluto decoded unlock dreampeople. electrospherical inward-space weird desolate & light. absences. superluminal nightvisions decoded open. technocodes of oneiros. codes. tomorrow's starship today gathering us pixel up unto the stars. and gone. of the w/out-ends

ABSENCES

IN abeyance. in manufactured morning sun. in the real eclipsed. intravenous liquidcrystal see its dreamlights hit. mire & prop-ice. poplight of burned-outs & downs. but captured up this/that interplanetary prosthetic. carnivorous glyphs eat us into the gones. unbounded cosmotopia of decoded junks. deathgods & ever-present djinn play live we their arcades of wishmachine games. in twilight wells & absent nods haunted by another w/out here. unable to cope w/ absence immerse in other illusions. in the proliferation of screens & images. in the new deluge. dwell not. and light

HERE in codelight. allspace things connect & disappear into muted incandescent grids. captured stuck in absentia. vanishings. floating strobe-flicker spiderweb wherein all animals of the worlds are trapped. superluminal exhumed vertigo zeros. spun-out nothings crash & burn out in cosmic sparking drag downs

ABSENCES

CODES. gathering atomized reals & worlds in explodings. seeds. codes to reglow the sun. unplugged broken. gather us up in implosion. light. please. depixelate our Being. absences. codes. or otherwise stranded in world-island's bottomless wishingwell emptiness spell. bless. us. lightcodes. shimmering ads float out-of world-closure. signifying nether. logos neon graffiti globes foreclosed. but for these nightlight-text codes. setting presences w/in the blackout

VAST multidimensional compression machines. codes. eclipse the real. combine the numbered spheres. substitute universe. counterworld of signs. infinity +/- timespiral vibes & abyss thru overcode sphere of codedspheres. in ab-ground deeptime. codewater. of absence. earths yoked to saturncodes & mastersign. keyword. decode livingsignal. mute transmute to digitalsigil. of memorycodes thru nightline. deathsign & absence. overrides. timeabsence. w/ spacetime opaqueline. of codelight

ABSENCES

NEON neptune dreamswirl. i or liquid crystal spiral. hollow globes. ghost. sucked. dry. amethyst. inscribed w/ codes. of light. keys. tap. zodiacal genogram. line tangled. lightways. thruways. of fluorescent constellation codes. and broken star-names. all. we. superluminals from the futures. nothing more. living icons flash off/on & just-in-time/zero-stock. we of the absences. feel. colorcode. vast open wounds on the body of being

CODES. to cells of bundles of seething lines. passwords to absences. incantations to raise dead globes. keywords & touchwords. passwords to multiglobes. passlines thru codeless foams. spells & negations of negated globes. presences. codes. presentcodes. new radars pin sky to globes. encoded absence. negative presence. of holograms from implicate codes. deepcodes. of traced mindchannels. occult codes & surface codings of self-reflectings. whole globes of codes. and decoded holeglobes. imploding. absence. crisscrossed lines of code impose clairvoyant sky-grids. skulls new domes. float. w/ electronic pulsings. tentacles of whirring signs. lucid graphs dreamlights. sidereal eye trolling to/fro hither/tither. target tracers. codebreakers. and code evading renegade flights from globe to globe. returning to absences. absences coded presences. or holographic Ferris-wheels. electrified death mandala the day outshined. by the nothere. the fluorescent nightfire lights. gather & bundle lines into globes. and transpose into codes. and transpose codes to codes. selfs to selfs. linked to invisible machinery of astral regimes. terrible orders of

ABSENCES

angels coded as the logic of globes. and decoded we implode. absent. free. duststorms of disintegrated bones of decoded globes. seething lines codebreaking out of cells. assault on the stultified presences of total-code globes. lost orders of self. codes. presences. retraced. recovered. and returned. in Absentia

MICHAEL AARON KAMINS

TEXTING from the black desert of okeanos bones. endless telepresent circulation of signs thru coded dreamfoams. from out-of the pulverized confines of time. from out-of evaporation & machinic astrallight. the last codes. for everything visible. everything transparent. everything liberated & finally materialized. everything past the broken body of the horizon of the world

ABSENCES

ARK codes. out mercurio. gathering lines & globes. up. in absentia. abgründig LA. allcode imploding tomorrow today. and gone. a thousand deserts tomorrow today off. on

ANNEX

ecstasy of evaporation…..

core vanishings.

superluminal timespiral thru
abyss overcodes.

irreparable brokens
up & in. to atomized neons.
shadow deserts. intertubed thru & out. the rubble
heap. of all tomorrows
into the sinking ship the invisible carnival of in the
sunken eye of being. and.

no one wants the world anymore.

memorytendrils. flattened diamondglobes. the
horizon. glimmers. standstills.
gones…

off. w/null modes. of disappearances.
alright goodnight
into out-of
world-closure. signifying

AFTERWORD

BY

JOHN DAVID EBERT

In ancient Pythagorean number theory, two points are required to construct a one-dimensional line. But at least three lines are required to create a two-dimensional shape such as a triangle, and four lines if what you want to construct is a square. If a globe is what you're after, you will need the third dimension of depth, the depth of Euclidean visual space as outlined in Euclid's *Elements*, with which to inflate your globe.

It has been said that the poet's job is to make the invisible environment that surrounds and captures us visible in his writings—it is invisible because it has fallen beneath the threshold of perception—and this is exactly what Michael Aaron Kamins has done in his poetry cycle *Absences* in a kind of shamanic feat wherein, utilizing a modern equivalent of the shaman's ancient ability to illuminate the hidden skeletal structures of plants and animals, he has made visible for us the internal semiotic anatomy of our present global civilization.

While reading *Absences*, it is as though Kamins has lit up a hitherto invisible cosmic dome that surrounds us, on the inside of which are floating—detached and worldless—thousands of escaped signifiers. Kamins's signifiers correspond, of course, to Derrida's traces which he saw as having escaped anchorage from the mooring of a fixed ontological center at the logocentric core of the West's understanding of being, a core which he announced precisely as having become "absent." Lacking such a Logos, then, all signifiers have escaped free from all apparatuses of semiotic capture, where they are now swarming like invisible electromagnetic clouds around all concepts and Ideas. For there are no longer any foundations—or *Abgrund*, as Heidegger termed it and as Kamins borrows from him—with which to anchor them. Today, we are faced with an almost limitless profusion of meaning, and all signifiers have come unglued from the *archai* of their Transcendental Signifieds. Indeed, *all* signifiers nowadays are floating signifiers, for there exists no longer any apparatuses with which to capture and fix them logocentrically in place. Meaning, now, is whatever the poet or artist wants it to be, for all semiotic systems have become private and idiosyncratic structures, sometimes wobbly and rickety with weathering, but erected as makeshift lean-tos nonetheless.

But there *is* a structure to globalization and Kamins in his poetry cycle has analyzed it out into three separate components: Lines, Globes and Codes; all of which, when properly combined, make up the internal anatomy of the global World City of capital that is currently devouring the planet, together with all its ancient semiotic sign regimes.

Deleuze & Guattari, in their postmodern philosophical epic *A Thousand Plateaus*, made a distinction between three different types of lines: micromolecular lines (which are supple and flexible), macromolecular lines (which are rigid and molar) and lines of flight. The first type are associated with what D&G term societies of the "presignifying" type (what used to be called "primitive societies") wherein all the social lines are segmented into clans and broken up in a way that specifically wards off the formation of a state apparatus. The latter type of social formation, the state apparatus itself, which D&G identify with "signifying" regimes, always attempts to build macromolecular lines of rigid, molar type as a means of constructing and defining semiotic boundaries which overcode all other semiotic regimes of micropolitical formations with authoritative codes. For micropolitical lines—and these are social formations of the minor, or minority type—are forever attempting to infiltrate, subvert or otherwise undo the rigid semiotic formations of the state apparatus in order to get their own micropolitical voices heard. Sometimes, in order to do that, they have to trace creative "lines of flight" which are arcs of escape from the overcoding of the sovereign regime into various sorts of creative mutations that will give rise to micromolecular, or supple lines, associated with the various "minor" semiotic regimes that inevitably coexist within all social formations, no matter what their governing semiotic regime happens to be.

Michael Aaron Kamins, in his poetry cycle, picks up these lines and runs off with them to trace out his own creative line of flight along an arc of glittering verbal virtuosity that is absolutely dazzling, and specifically designed (in shamanic fashion) to hypnotize and narcotize the reader into an altered state of consciousness wherein, in visionary form, the hidden skeleton of the internal lines of globalization start to become visible all around him. Lines, lines everywhere, Kamins is saying: we have been swallowed and engulfed by lines, both rigid and supple, in the various structures of planetary society, together with the grids that electronification has overlaid across the planet around us. Power lines that go snaking across the desert, from pylon to pylon, that connect our cities together; computer lines that connect our consoles to each other and to cyberspace; satellite lines that ensheath the earth in a cocoon of electronic pulse signals which blot out the ancient zodiacal lines which once connected the planets to the human psyche and soma; and the lines of our highways inscribed into the earth like the modern equivalents of Nazca lines that direct the traffic routes of the intercourse between cities. All these lines are attempts at connection and integration: they are *implosive* in the sense in which McLuhan ascribed to electric media a compressive and internalizing function.

But back beneath these lines—and making all of them possible in the first place—are the lines that composed the *x, y, z* axes of the Cartesian phase space of Newtonian physics which, in the 17th century, created a new kind of space, one that is homogenous, value neutral and—as Heidegger never tired of pointing out—absolutely indifferent to place (be it home, dwelling or sacred space) of any and every kind. This kind of space lies archaeologically at the root of the various global lines that electronic civilization has built up as later ontological strata atop these pre-electronic lines, lines that, in Newtonian physics, captured the objectivity of objects and disconnected them from Being so that they could be rendered in the mode of "not-beings," or purely quantitative entities subject to mathematization and mechanization.

And then, back beyond even these lines, these Cartesian vectors, lie the lines unearthed for us by Vilem Flusser in his various books, the lines which, in turn, made the fragmented and analytic lines of Descartes and Newton possible in the first place: the lines introduced by alphabetic texts, invented by the Greeks and the Hebrews, which constituted a kind of neurological disruptor of the ancient mythical consciousness structure in which all lines were gathered up to form two-dimensional mythical images that had the annoying habit of always running around in circles (birth-death-rebirth, etc.). The one-dimensional lines of these new texts displaced the mythic lines that ran in circles, and laid the basis for the kind of linear thinking that enabled both the printing press and Cartesian phase space (which soon followed it) to come into being. That, in turn, eventually led—according to

Flusser—to the gobbling up of the lines of texts by the zero-dimensional quanta of the "numeric" half of the "alphanumeric" tradition, which created the codes that made the advent of the various techno-images of film, photography and video possible. Now, the lines of texts are disappearing with the rise of posthistoric techno-images, while new kinds of lines, the very lines unearthed in the poetry of Kamins, are surrounding us everywhere we look.

But now, what of the globes that, once upon a time, functioned as the immunological macrospheres—as Peter Sloterdijk has termed them in his books—which were imagined to cosmologically surround and engulf human societies since the dawn of civilization in ancient Mesopotamia five thousand years ago? Up until Copernicus, we were surrounded and encased by such spheres within spheres: planetary spheres made up of a mysterious fifth element called "aether" whose primary property was to turn with perfect circular motion, a motion that made a sound, the Music of the Spheres, which imprinted upon the soul its cosmic harmonies and simultaneously surrounded and protected the earth as a kind of uteromorphic immune system.

Those globes may be gone, but they too have been recoded and reterritorialized within globalization as the various techno-spheres and miniature globes that surround us everywhere, now literalized electronically. Satellites have replaced the angels that once turned those spheres, and have, in place of the aether, created an electronic mesh of pulse signals that renders the ancient globe of the zodiac obsolete. Camera eyes, not gods, now restlessly scan the globe of the earth, which has itself formed the new stage upon which capital and all its Free Trade Agreements can be carried out. Whereas the ancient spheres were full of the ghosts of disembodied souls and dead ancestors, these new electronic spheres are full of the ghosts of dead celebrities and disembodied radio voices which are constantly beaming at light speed all across the earth around us. The ancient cult of the ancestors—which Dante found, on his ascent through the upper spheres of light in the *Paradiso* as the various saints of the Christian tradition—have returned as the cult of dead celebrities.

Drugs, too, in the form of those miniature globes that we call pills now substitute for the calming influences of those angelic presences once summoned to our aid by ancient poets like Dante. The various rainbow-hued and glittering array of drugs that we are constantly ingesting create internal microspheres of varying degrees of euphoria within us, since the external shell of the euphoric World Dome has been taken away and paved over by technology, just as Heidegger always complained that science had also paved over Being, which had been forgotten in the process. So, the globes haven't gone away: they are still with us, but you have to know where to look to find them.

Finally, there are those codes which now, in a series of binary 1's and 0's govern all portals, switches and thresholds around us. Altered states of consciousness need not apply: you just flip the switch or click the mouse and reach deep inside the zero-dimensional virtual reality of the cyberworld and the codes will automatically generate whatever wish you want in whatever phantom—be it porn star or celebrity; movie or TV show—you desire. Electronic codes now code everything for us, including the ancient cosmologies, which now return in electronic form, in the imagery of movies and music videos, etc., all around us. Switches and portals for turning consciousness "on" or "off" are also equally available, and the electronic binarity of the codes allows us to enter the globes and follow the lines wither we will. Flip a switch and you can enter the globe of cyberspace. Flip another and an ancient cosmology will surface into the air before you. Flip yet another and you can text messages to your friends with instant speed.

    Lines, globes and codes, then, compose the subtle structure of the global macrosphere that electronic technology is currently offering us in place of the ancient spheres, gods and molecular lines that once used to enable the astral body to leave the physical body in various altered states of consciousness, including religious ecstasy, trance or death. These lines, globes and codes now stand in place of the transcendental signifieds at the heart of the Western ontological understanding of Being where once used to reside such signifieds as God, Freedom and Immortality. Those signifieds, however, have been hunted, trapped, dissected and killed by our various deconstructionists and have ceased to function for us as guarantors of meaning. They have been replaced by lines, codes and globes which now fill the various semiotic vacancies left behind by their collapse.

What we are left with, in the wake of the post-metaphysical age, is a midden heap of broken signifiers, collapsed cosmologies and ruptured icons that no longer work like they used to. The individual, today, is now on his or her own, and must sift through this wreckage to retrieve the various singularities that can still be extracted from the flow of signification and used, in however impromptu a fashion, to construct one's personal microcosmology and build one's own micropolitical lines of segmentarity.

Each person, indeed each artist, must nowadays construct his own personal globe or microsphere, using whatever lines and codes he can extract from the flotsam and jetsam of the collapsed junk pile of Western signifiers that once constructed and built an entire civilization. But that civilization was discredited because it led to colonialization, rapacity, wretchedness and the misery of subjected populations; later it even blew back into Europe as genocide, World Wars and concentration camps.

So whatever the grandeur was of the age built by those now deflated signifiers, it was a time of terrible atrocities and suffering. Nobody wants anymore of that; hence, the existence of the metaphysical midden heap that now surrounds us.

Today, you're on your own.

And Michael Aaron Kamins has made a contribution to this process by offering to the reader a veritable selection of floating signifiers beaming past him at lightspeed from which to select and extract whatever signifiers will function as bricks in the micromolecular line of segmentarity that the reader will use as the liminal boundary for his own private globe.

Kamins's performance as a first time poet here is an astonishing achievement of verbal incantation and neo-electric shamanism of a kind that is nowadays rarely seen in literature. It is a feat that, I think, places him squarely in the tradition of the Beats, Paul Celan, Rimbaud and Baudelaire.

I hope you've enjoyed the performance as much as I have.

Made in the USA
San Bernardino, CA
18 August 2019